Praise for *Winter Meditations*

Following the natural rhythm of the seasons,
Fr. John Bartunek invites readers to return to
their roots with these insightful and meditative
reflections. Weaving together the personal style
of memoir with the unifying universality of our
faith, Fr. Bartunek's *Winter Meditations* offers us
a good reminder to embrace silence, to be still, to
experience hope, to know wisdom, to recognize
grace in the world around us, and to continue
working on our relationship with God.

—Daniel P. Horan, OFM,
visiting assistant professor
at Catholic Theological Union (Chicago) and
author of *God Is Not Fair and Other Reasons for Gratitude*

This book invites you to lay aside your dread of
winter and appreciate both its necessity in the
natural world and its spiritual benefits.

—Barb Szyszkiewicz, OFS,
writer at FranciscanMom.com
and editor of CatholicMom.com

D1115173

Winter meditations

JOHN BARTUNEK, LC, SThD

Liguori

Imprimi Potest:
Stephen T. Rehrauer, CSsR, Provincial
Denver Province, the Redemptorists
Imprimi Potest:
Fr. John Connor, LC, Territorial Director
Territory of Northern America, Legionaries of Christ
Published by Liguori Publications
Liguori, Missouri 63057
To order, visit Liguori.org or call 800-325-9521.

Library of Congress Cataloging-in-Publication Data

Names: Bartunek, John, author.5Title: Winter meditations / John Bartunek, LC SThD.
Description: First Edition. | Liguori : Liguori Publications, 2016.
Identifiers: LCCN 2016041515 (print) | LCCN 2016044085 (ebook) |
ISBN 9780764825644 | ISBN 9780764870156 ()
Subjects: LCSH: Winter—Religious aspects—Christianity--Meditations. |
Spiritual exercises.
Classification: LCC BV135.W56 B37 2016 (print) | LCC BV135.W56 (ebook)
| DDC
242—dc23
LC record available at https://lccn.loc.gov/2016041515

Liguori Publications, a nonprofit corporation, is an apostolate of the Redemptorists. To learn more about the Redemptorists, visit Redemptorists.com.

Printed in the United States of America

20 19 18 17 16 / 5 4 3 2 1

First Edition

✳

Contents

7   **Introduction**

11   **Chapter 1:** *Silence*

19   **Chapter 2:** *Sacrifice*

29   **Chapter 3:** *Stillness*

37   **Chapter 4:** *Prudence*

47   **Chapter 5:** *Waiting*

55 **Chapter 6:** *Perseverance*

65 **Chapter 7:** *Hope*

75 **Chapter 8:** *Companionship*

83 **Chapter 9:** *Benevolence*

93 **Chapter 10:** *Truth*

101 **Chapter 11:** *Generosity*

109 **Chapter 12:** *Grace*

Introduction

We don't need scientific studies to tell us today's culture is out of touch with nature, even though plenty of such studies are available. Not only are various social pockets engaged in industrial activities that have dangerous effects on the environment, but also few of us postmodern people are able to live our lives in harmony with the natural rhythms of the earth.

In fact, we tend to ignore them, whether consciously or not. We can make daytime seem like nighttime and nighttime seem like daytime. We can make winter feel like summer and summer feel like winter. We can travel from the tropics to the tundra in less than a day, from the mountains to the sea in an afternoon. We can find whatever fruits or vegetables we want in our local grocery store, regardless of whether they are supposed to be in season or out of season.

Our natural environment has become a kind of add-on to our lives. We feel the pangs of weather changes and the panic of natural disasters. As of yet we haven't learned to control such things with technology, but our day-to-day, month-to-month, and year-to-year lives have, in general, gotten out of synch with the natural rhythms of the earth we were created to live in.

This can cause problems. As human beings, our lives are *meant* to unfold in harmony with the natural world. The seasons, the processes of nature, the *rhythms* of this world—our world—were created out of love and given to us as a home. They have something to tell us about our deeper identities, the purpose of our lives, the way to live our lives to the full. When we cut ourselves off from direct, regular, and necessary contact with and dependence on this natural environment, we threaten to sever an ancient and irreplaceable link to authentic wisdom. This is why I decided to write these meditations.

A Needed Return to Natural Wisdom

The bite-sized chapters in these books (this is the fourth of four, each dedicated to one of the four natural seasons) will provide you with some space to remember and reconnect with this essential dimension of your humanity. That is what meditation means: giving yourself the time and space, both physically and psychologically, to reflect calmly but deeply on some of our more important spiritual values. It is my sincere hope that by doing so you will experience a spiritual and emotional revitalization. You will be able to escape from the ceaseless, inhuman, digitalized grind of post-modern life and regain balance.

Not that I am accusing you of being unspiritual. I'm banking on the fact that even though you have faith, hope, courage, and love, you still feel a hunger to have *more* of them—deeper faith, more vibrant hope, more dynamic courage, stronger love. That's one of the great things about spiritual values. Because they are spiritual, they can always keep growing.

Avoiding the Rush

This volume only contains twelve meditations, one for each week of the season. But at the end of each meditation I have included suggested activities to help you absorb the nourishing truths that the meditation explained in the "Making It Your Own" sections. A good way to use this book is to read a meditation at the beginning of the week, underlining, highlighting, and writing in the margins as you reflect on what you read. Then for the rest of the week, take time each day to review your highlights and to put into practice one of the suggested activities. Following that method will assure that whatever good ideas you find as you read will have sufficient time and space to seep from your mind into your heart and your spirit, fostering personal renewal.

Getting Personal

These meditations contain many personal anecdotes that I think help illustrate my points. I also hope that making myself vulnerable in this way will encourage you to reflect on the richness of your own life experience to find the lessons, the nuggets of wisdom, that God, in his generous providence, always offers to you.

May this volume of simple meditations on the season of winter be a window through which you can discover, once again, the "dearest freshness deep down things"[1] that have always nourished what is best in the human spirit.

---

[1] From Gerard Manley Hopkins' poem "God's Grandeur"

Chapter 1: *Silence*

Is anything as silent as a country landscape after a heavy snowfall? When the wind dies down, the clouds scatter, the morning sun glints off the crystals of freshly fallen snow, and the whole world is hushed. But the hush isn't fearful or anxious. It is a hush of contentment, fullness, and satisfaction. It is like the silence that comes to a child who crawls under warm covers after a day of playing outside in the snow, a sigh of quiet happiness that accompanies a gentle smile as the little soul drifts off to sleep. The hush that comes upon a winter's day after a fresh snowfall is the sigh of quiet happiness and the gentle smile of a world at rest.

Do you remember hearing and feeling this hush? Do you remember bundling up in a thick coat and heavy boots, in mittens and scarves, then venturing outside into that winter wonderland? Stepping into the sacred silence. Making the first footprints. Do you remember?

It may not be easy to recall. Our world has become noisy. Audible noise, visual noise, and mental noise have become such constant companions that many people flee from silence. If, through an unlikely coincidence, silence surprises us, we panic. We whip out a smartphone and turn up the volume.

Is our noisiness a good thing? After all, summer is natural, but it's noisy. Spring, too, has its noise. Noise has a place in the rhythm of the seasons. But so does silence. So does the quiet hush of a fresh snowfall.

I have always been an introvert. I value and am energized by alone time. So I was surprised when I entered religious life and discovered that, up to that point, my life had been exceedingly, unhealthily noisy.

In the novitiate, which comprise the first two years of religious formation, we follow a monastic regimen. The reasoning behind it is simple. A religious novice is attempting to discern whether or not God is calling him to a life of vowed poverty, chastity, and obedience. Discerning that call involves patiently sifting through the often-hidden motivations behind a young man's desire to become a religious priest. The environment of silence allows interior noise to settle and subside, like white flakes in an agitated snow globe after it is set down again.

A religious novice is also being introduced to a more intense spiritual life. This involves hours spent in prayer each day. It requires developing one's faith and interior sensitivity to discern the voice of the Lord. Silence fosters the development of this spiritual sensitivity and becomes a training ground for the self-discipline required to maintain interior silence later on, when the priest is sent back into the noisy world.

I liked the auditory silence. It was easy for me, as a thoughtful—maybe even brooding—introvert. What stunned and disoriented me was the visual silence. Television and movies were reserved for exceptional moments and limited to religious subjects. The images on the walls inside the cloister were few and consisted entirely of devotional content. We all wore the same religious habit and had the same haircut. You can imagine what a contrast it was to live in that kind of environment following years at the university and work in a major metropolis.

I felt keenly the lack of visual stimuli that had been my daily bread ever since I could remember: the nonstop bombardment of advertisers; the ebullient abundance of shapes and colors everywhere you look; the variety of clothing styles and colors; the incessant change of scenery as you move from home, to work, to the gym, to the store, to the mall, to a friend's house. All that was simply unplugged.

What was the result? Surprising freedom. My sensory experience felt unshackled. I began to notice things I had never paid attention to before: the vibrancy of colors in the garden; the textures of tree trunks and stone and marble; the fragrances of the different seasons and of the weather changes; the taste of simple foods and water; the weight of humidity and the feel of the air I breathed as the temperature fluctuated.

When on liturgical feast days we would whip out the special vestments during Mass, listen to music in free time, or prepare something special for our meals, the sights and sounds and flavors would fill my senses in a way they didn't before. The noise of the world around me no longer drowned out the music of God's creation and providence. It was like being born again.

This experience isn't exclusive to my vocation. It is an experience we can all enjoy and that God wants us all to enjoy. God has so much he wants to say to us! Silence creates space for us to hear him better.

The prophet Elijah learned this lesson after a dramatic battle with the evil Queen Jezebel, which led him to flee to the wilderness and take refuge in a cave. There he waited for the Lord to show him what to do. Here is what happened next:

...A great and powerful wind tore the mountains apart and shattered the rocks before the Lord, but the Lord was not in the wind. After the wind there was an earthquake, but the Lord was not in the earthquake. After the earthquake came a fire, but the Lord was not in the fire. And after the fire came a gentle whisper. When Elijah heard it, he pulled his cloak over his face and went out and stood at the mouth of the cave. Then a voice said to him, "What are you doing here, Elijah?"

1 Kings 19:11–13,
New International Version

God wasn't in the chaos and the noise of the earthquake and wind. He was in the quiet whisper. This is how the Lord speaks to us.

Silence is necessary for hearing. Lovers prefer quiet corners for heart-to-heart exchanges. Amidst the din of a crowd they cannot hear the words they wish to speak to each other. Likewise, for us to hear the words of wisdom and love that the Lord wishes to whisper to us, we need to weave silence into our lives.

We all need to make room for silence in our lives. Sometimes, we all need to put on our mittens and earmuffs and venture out into the pure hush of a landscape blanketed in fresh snow. That kind of silence is part of the gift of winter, a gift with surprising, delightful benefits.

Making It Your Own

† Choose one sentence from this chapter that really resonated in your heart or compose a one-sentence summary. Write it on a sticky note. Put it where you will see it throughout the week as a reminder that, in an overly noisy world, silence has a lot to say.

† Take one day this week and go entirely offline —no internet, no messaging, no calls. Unplug from the noise of the digital continent for a day and see what happens. Write down your experience in a journal.

† Arrange a long family meal this week or sometime soon—include hors d'oeuvres at the beginning and tea or coffee at the end. Make it a requirement that everyone has to leave phones in a basket by the front door. Enjoy each other's presence without interruptions. Reflect on what the experience showed you.

† There is a long tradition of fasting in Christian spirituality. Fasting is a wise way to rein in certain mental or physical habits that have grown out of control. This week, fast from one source of "noise" in your life that detracts from your ability to live in the present moment. Reflect on the effects this has by writing about them in your journal.

† Throughout this week, begin your daily prayer with an exercise in silence. Simply close your eyes and listen to the ambient sounds, identifying them one by one. Or, keep your eyes open and simply gaze at what is in front of you. Do this for two or three minutes before you begin praying. Notice what effect it has on your prayer and why.

Chapter 2: *Sacrifice*

Although seasonal changes happen more noticeably in places farther from the equator, they affect the entire biosphere. A villager who lives near the Amazon River's delta may never feel the frosty touch of a snowflake, but if winter were to disappear, the villager would find out quickly enough.

Life needs winter. As our spinning globe orbits the sun, its tilt brings one hemisphere into a more direct path of receiving the solar rays (summer), while the other hemisphere receives them less directly (winter). As a result, less light and warmth reaches us in winter. Seasonal snow makes its appearance, painting a wintry landscape. Winter also affects the cryosphere, the polar regions where water exists almost exclusively in its solid forms of snow and ice.

In the wonderfully complex and intricate interdependence of terrestrial territories, cold and snow become critical contributors to many of the world's most abundant crop-growing areas. The amount of snow that accumulates on certain mountain ranges and the length of its stay significantly impact water levels for agricultural activity during the rest of the year. These mountainous regions become the water buckets for their symbiotic agrarian breadbaskets. Without winter being winter, summer can't be summer. Winter isn't just a frigid pause in the life cycles of the natural seasons. It's necessary.

Spiritual winters play a role in the seasons of our spiritual growth. These come to all of us, wherever we live in relation to the equator. We have to decide how we will react to them. Spiritual winters are seasons of suffering, sorrow, and loss. A frost seems to settle on the relationship between a husband and wife, or an old friendship becomes cold and brittle. Or employment flags and a whole family finds itself struggling to survive, and tensions build in the home and in each heart. A wintry chill may descend upon our life of prayer and piety, and God may seem to have turned his back on us. No matter how fervently we seek him, all we find are cold memories and shards of broken icicles where there used to be a warm fire of faith-filled intimacy.

Sometimes these spiritual winters are brought on by our own sins. In these cases, winter may last much longer than it should. Humble repentance is the only remedy for those winters. We have to turn back to the light and leave the darkness behind us.

Other times, our spiritual winters are governed by the same providence that guides the rhythms of nature. In those circumstances, we need to learn how to accept the loss and integrate it into our identity. This takes faith. This takes what spiritual writers have long called the *discipline of sacrifice.* Just as the earth must temporarily release its hold on the burgeoning fruitfulness of summer for winter to arrive and make its essential contribution, so, too, the Lord often asks us to release our grip on some of the good things of life so he can, eventually, pour even better things into our laps. Giving things up for God and his eternal kingdom is the heart of sacrifice. When we do so out of faith and love, a spiritual water bucket can result that irrigates the fertile plains of our heart.

When I travel, I almost always wear my Roman collar. You never know when someone may need to speak to a priest, so wearing a priestly collar is like wearing a spiritual "open for business" sign. Sometimes this leads to deep and gratifying conversations. Other times it leads to insults. More frequently it sparks brief exchanges in which the most common question is: "Why aren't Catholic priests allowed to get married?"

Lifelong celibacy is the most obvious sacrifice a priest or other consecrated person makes. Priestly celibacy has various reasons: priests are spiritually married to the Church; priests are following Christ's own example of celibate service; priests are called by God to be signs of the world to come....I was aware of those reasons when discerning my own priestly vocation, and I accepted them. But what I didn't know was how much I would receive as a result of accepting the call. I, like all priests, have given up the possibility of having an intimate marital relationship and the possibility of having biological children of my own. And yet, through the years my priesthood has been a dynamic source of spiritual intimacy and spiritual fatherhood.

Because of his celibacy, a priest belongs to God in a special way. As a result, he also belongs to God's people in a special way. They are able to open their hearts and souls to a priest in ways they cannot with anyone else. God works through that relationship, pouring his grace through the priest into that person's life.

Once, in the Denver airport waiting not-so-patiently for a delayed flight, I found a quiet corner and began to pray my rosary, walking back and forth with my eyes lowered. As I made the turn during the first decade, I found myself face to face with a middle-aged woman whose eyes were filled with pain. She approached me without my noticing. When I looked at her, she asked, with a trembling voice: "Will you please pray with me?"

I was surprised but could see she was suffering profoundly. I said, "Of course." We bowed our heads and I began to pray for her. After a minute or so, it occurred to me that there was probably something in particular on her mind. I interrupted my prayer and looked up to ask her. She was weeping. I asked her if there was something in particular she wanted to pray about, and she answered between sobs: "My mother. My mother just died."

Her sadness was total. It had a dark, hopeless cast to it. My heart broke. We both bowed our heads again while I prayed for the eternal repose of her mother's soul.

When I finished, I made the sign of the cross and looked up, hoping to offer her words of comfort. But she spoke first. "Thank you," she said. Her face was still wet with tears, but the hopelessness in her eyes had been replaced by the light of peace and relief.

I never knew her name. I never saw her again. Yet I know our encounter was a moment of supernatural grace. God touched her heart in an indescribably meaningful way through the simple prayer of his priest. It was one occasion when the Lord allowed me to glimpse and to taste the fruits that he is producing through the sacrifice involved in my following his call.

The etymological root of the word *sacrifice* means "to make holy" *(sacrum facere)*. Holiness is the quality of fulfillment that God's presence brings. Whenever God asks us to give something up out of faith and love, to accept a loss or endure a suffering that is outside of our control but not outside the reach of his providence, we can be sure that something good will come of it. Winters are necessary for summers to flourish.

Jesus often taught this law of sacrifice. It is, at least in part, what has traditionally been meant by "taking up" one's cross:

> ...Whoever does not take up his cross and follow after me is not worthy of me. Whoever finds his life will lose it, and whoever loses his life for my sake will find it....Give and gifts will be given to you; a good measure, packed together, shaken down, and overflowing, will be poured into your lap. For the measure with which you measure will in return be measured out to you.
>
> *Matthew 10:38–39; Luke 6:38*

We need not fear winter. Winter has its own beauty, mysterious and undeniable. Winter is necessary. When loss and sorrow come our way, let's call to mind this lesson that God has taught us in Jesus and that he continues to teach us with every first snow of the year.

Making It Your Own

✝ Choose one sentence from this chapter that really resonated in your heart or compose a one-sentence summary. Write it on a sticky note. Put it where you will see it throughout the week as a reminder that faith-filled sacrifice is a necessary and productive aspect of life in this fallen world.

✝ Take time this week to remember your most vivid experiences of winter. Which of your winters has been the most memorable? Why? Reflect on them, recall them, maybe even write down detailed descriptions of them. Use this exercise to help solidify your conviction that winters—of whatever sort—are not outside of God's providence.

✝ Try to remember a time when someone sacrificed to help or benefit you. What were the circumstances? How did it turn out? Thank God for that gift, and thank the person who sacrificed for you.

† Reflect on your own experiences of making sacrifices out of faith and love. How did those sacrifices make you feel, and why? What results did those sacrifices produce? How do you think God sees them?

† Sometimes we become frustrated or angry when we make a sacrifice and don't receive the return we were hoping for. Why is that? How did Jesus react when his sacrifice wasn't accepted by many of the people he came to save? What can you learn from that?

Chapter 3: *Stillness*

We have the impression that the earth sleeps underneath its winter blanket of snow. We tend to think of that sleep as a dormancy of life, a passive waiting for spring and vitality. Yet any healthy sleep is more than passive waiting. Animals, including humans, need sleep. Sleep rejuvenates us physically and psychologically. When we close our eyes and curl up for a night of rest, we withdraw from exterior activity and allow interior replenishment to happen. After a good night's sleep, we awake refreshed. Something happened to us. Revitalization took place from the inside out and never could have happened any other way.

Something similar happens to the soil during the winter months. In the spring and summer, the ground swells with fresh vitality. But that flow of new life was being prepared throughout the long winter of apparent stillness and withdrawal.

Winter is the season when the remnants of aboveground life surrender themselves to the earth. Instead of pushing life up and out, the soil pulls back and the chemical and biological elements recede and go to work under the blanket of snow. The blossoming of springtime is the morning wake-up of an earth replenished by the hidden but vital processes of winter's frosty cover.

For our spirits to flourish, for our capacity for creativity and virtue to thrive, we must experience periods of external stillness and apparent inactivity. To stay healthy and energetic in our external activities, we must allow ourselves times of contemplation, of unhurried thought and reflection.

Winter is an icon of this kind of deep thought. Its stillness, even starkness, belies a hidden fruitfulness being prepared in the depths of the earth. We also have hidden depths in our minds and souls. But if we never give ourselves time for reflection and thoughtful observation, the fruitfulness will be easily depleted and we will feel scattered, overextended, and spiritually anemic.

Sometimes summer crops thrive before the midsummer solstice, but their growth loses momentum afterward. Even chemical fertilizers can't always jump-start this kind of sputtering. The soil simply lacks sufficient vitality. Its winter failed to supply enough replenishment, like a poor night's sleep.

When we mindlessly follow the frenetic pace of postmodern life, working hard to get the competitive edge, filling our free time with activity after activity, and bombarding ourselves with external stimuli during our recreation, the soil of our souls can easily become depleted. We are not meant to be plugged in 24/7. Our spiritual summers depend upon the hidden processes of interior renewal that occur through relaxed thought and contemplation, through periodically withdrawing from external activity to reflect on what's happening interiorly.

I have written before about my junior year of college, which I spent overseas studying history in Italy and Poland. It was a year full of special graces for me. One of them came while I was spending the first part of my Christmas vacation in Assisi, the mystical medieval city that gave the world St. Francis and St. Clare. At that point I was not yet a Catholic. My art history professor had arranged for me to spend a week in the Franciscan novitiate there, living with the young novices. I could have spent that vacation traveling from city to city, skiing or otherwise socializing and enjoying the youthful high life. But something moved me to retreat from the typical collegiate escapades. I needed space to think, pray, and look inward.

I befriended a retired American priest during my stay, a man whose wisdom and humility began to break down my prejudices and misconceptions about Catholicism. That dismantling was not comfortable. It threw me for a loop. I experienced painful moments of interior turbulence. One night I was so agitated that I couldn't fall asleep. So I made my way to the chapel and spent an extended time in prayer, wrestling with the Lord in my efforts to understand and accept what he was doing in my heart. His grace touched me that night. It filled me with peace, joy, and hope. I went back to bed and slept soundly.

I awoke the next morning to see the courtyard of the monastery covered in a pristine mantle of fresh snow. It rarely snows in Assisi, and when it does, the snow doesn't usually accumulate. There in the courtyard I looked upon a marvelous idyll. I spent the whole morning outside gazing and rejoicing in the beauty of it, the captivating purity of this new-fallen snow. I knew it was a message from my Lord: *I am giving you a new beginning here, a fresh spiritual start, and it is going to lead you on a glorious journey....*I had given a few days to stillness and contemplation, to prayer and self-reflection, and God had responded with graces that changed the direction of my life.

I have always found God to be exceedingly generous. Whenever I extract myself from hyperactivity to give space to quiet contemplation, the Lord gives me more than I can imagine. God's consistent generosity has strengthened my conviction about the value of stillness in our lives, expressed eloquently by the psalmist:

> Unless the Lord build the house,
> They labor in vain who build...
> It is vain for you to rise early
>   and put off your rest at night,
> To eat bread earned by hard toil—
>   all this God gives to his beloved
>   in sleep.
>
> *Psalm 127:1–2*

One ancient Greek philosopher famously quipped, "The unexamined life is not worth living." Unfortunately, popular culture seems to be built around avoiding calm and contemplative space to examine one's life. If we want to recover our true spiritual creativity, both as individuals and as a society, we must recover a capacity for stillness. We must rediscover the ancient Pauline wisdom that enjoins us to think frequently and deeply about "whatever is true, whatever is honorable, whatever is just, whatever is pure, whatever is lovely, whatever is gracious..." (Philippians 4:8). Perhaps we can begin by contemplating the example of the Lord himself, the most spiritually creative man whoever walked this earth, who would "withdraw to deserted places to pray" (Luke 5:16).

Making It Your Own

† Choose one sentence from this chapter that really resonated in your heart or compose a one-sentence summary. Write it on a sticky note. Put it where you will see it throughout the week as a reminder that stillness is a necessary ingredient in true and dependable creativity.

† Take time this week to reflect on the most creative periods in your life. What sparked them? What sustained them? What ended them? Then reflect on the least creative periods of your life. Write down the lessons you learn from this exercise and apply them to your current rhythm of life.

† List all the contemplative moments you have in a typical week. Are you satisfied with them? Are there enough of them? Are they substantial enough? If so, be grateful you have been given wisdom in this area. If not, decide prayerfully what you will do to create more contemplative space in your life.

† The fine arts (painting, music, drama, sculpture, architecture, dance) are fields of natural contemplation. They are spaces where beauty, truth, and goodness are explored, savored, and reflected upon. What role do the fine arts play in your life? What role would you like them to play?

† Think about the people you know and identify one friend or family member who has been especially busy and burdened lately. How can you help that soul have some healthy relaxation this week? Commit yourself to doing that out of love and respect for that person. Pray for strength and guidance to fulfill your commitment.

Chapter 4: *Prudence*

Before grocery stores and speedy shipping, people had to store up supplies to make it through the winter. Plenty of work went into pickling vegetables for the family and amassing feed for the livestock. Chopping wood, bolstering roofs and walls, and collecting wax or kerosene for indoor lighting required a lot of planning and much sweat. Once winter arrived, folks had to make intelligent use of the resources gathered. People had to make sure that what was gathered would last until spring. This involved thinking ahead, learning from experience, and exercising self-control. Surviving winter's challenges demanded practical wisdom, otherwise known as prudence.

The winter months brought a lot of work, too, of course: indoor work—sewing and weaving, carving and tinkering, carpentering and repairing—as well as outdoor work like hunting, skinning, clearing snow, and caring for the animals. Winter work was rarely glamorous, but it was necessary to prepare for a fruitful summer, just as summer work was necessary to prepare for winter survival.

The seasons complement each other. Recognizing the needs and seizing the opportunities of each requires humble attentiveness to reality and willingness to do what needs to be done, not just what we feel like doing. This, too, is an ingredient in the virtue of prudence, that intangible ability to choose the right means to achieve good ends.

Our popular culture's tendency to ignore seasonal rhythms—which we can do when we work in an office instead of on a farm and have central heating and electric lighting instead of a hearth and candles—distances us from reality and enervates our capacity for self-mastery. Survival no longer depends on prudence, and so healthy prudence has often been shelved in favor of overwork, overindulgence, and overstimulation.

This is a big loss, both for our culture and for our individual lives. Prudence may no longer be so necessary for mere survival, but it continues to be necessary for authentic fulfillment. Imprudence, making foolhardy decisions, and living by whims instead of wisdom lead to destruction and regret. Although life has its lighthearted side, and although Hollywood happy endings are entertaining and sometimes inspiring, true happiness doesn't come to us by chance or a wish. A truly happy life is built up day after day by meeting each challenge and opportunity with rational good sense and persevering determination.

Prudence is a virtue that helps us avoid sin. Sin is often attractive. It seems to award a short-term advantage to its victims. But sin is sin because it is bad for us. It offends God because it distances us from the lasting goodness he created us to experience. Sin always causes damage.

As a priest, I see this truth played out over and over again. When repentant sinners come to seek forgiveness in the confessional, when wounded spouses come to spiritual direction for advice and guidance, when aching hearts finally open up and look for healing after decades of bearing hidden regrets, I see the destructive flood of unnecessary suffering that sin always unleashes.

A few years ago, I was on an annual eight-day spiritual retreat. As I unpacked my suitcase, I noticed a folded piece of paper that had fallen between the wall and the prie-dieu (the kneeler used for prayer). I picked up the paper and didn't see any name on it, so I unfolded it. A few handwritten lines were scrawled there in blue ink. Here is what they said:

How can you love me? I have always been selfish—Only because you tried to love with your own heart. Yes, your heart is selfish, but my heart is not....I don't believe that my life is worth living. I have just failed the whole time and not gotten anywhere. What is the point? I'll just have the fun I can along the way, but nothing will ever come of it. I have been a terrible brother, son, uncle, brother-in-law, friend. I don't care about anyone but me.

As I read those anguished words, written by someone I had never met, my mind was filled with the memory of many others I had met who also felt the sting of moral failure and meaninglessness. I sat there in my room at the retreat center and prayed for whoever had written those lines and for all the others. I prayed for God's spirit of wisdom to find them. I prayed for his infinite mercy to touch and renew them and give them the fresh start that Jesus came to offer each of us as often as we need it. I don't remember the specific words I prayed, but I do remember that their meaning echoed the prayer to Jesus that we offer, repeatedly, in every Mass: "Lamb of God, who takes away the sins of the world, have mercy on us...."

Prudence requires both knowing where authentic happiness is to be found and making choices that lead us toward it. The Lord has mercifully revealed that our fulfillment comes from living in communion with God and that following the teachings and example of Jesus is the path wherein that communion unfolds. He does not just show us the way but pours his own divine grace into our souls to strengthen us on our journey.

Temptations still abound. Our fallen nature, the seductions of this world, and the snares of our ancient enemy, the devil, all tug at our hearts and constantly invite us to throw those gifts of faith to the wind. They put forth the idols of power, popularity, and pleasure as deceptive sources of happiness and life goals. They cajole us into relegating the sure but gentle voice of prudence to a distant corner of our minds while we bask in passing delights and achievements that promise much but never deliver.

Jesus assures us we are not mere victims. If we hear his words, we have the freedom to abide by them, as hard as it may seem. In fact, he concluded his famous Sermon on the Mount with a short parable that serves as a shining icon of prudence:

Everyone who listens to these words of mine and acts on them will be like a wise man who built his house on rock. The rain fell, the floods came, and the winds blew and buffeted the house. But it did not collapse; it had been set solidly on rock. And everyone who listens to these words of mine but does not act on them will be like a fool who built his house on sand. The rain fell, the floods came, and the winds blew and buffeted the house. And it collapsed and was completely ruined.

Matthew 7:24–27

What foundation are we building our lives on? Maybe by listening a bit more attentively to the lessons of the seasons, by paying more attention to the reality of God's creation and not just man-made noise, we will have a better chance to build well, to build on rock, to enjoy the sure and steady progress promised by prudence.

Sin is real and it is destructive. The humble attentiveness and inner strength that accompany prudence help us steer clear of sin and selfishness so we can truly flourish. Prudence reminds us life is not a mere and pointless game but a gift to be treasured, an opportunity to be cherished, an invitation to be accepted. Prudence reminds us we are called and enabled to be creative and responsible stewards of our own lives and of the world around us. It reminds us that responsibility is not an obstacle to lasting happiness. It is the very marrow of happiness.

Making It Your Own

† Choose one sentence from this chapter that really resonated in your heart or compose a one-sentence summary. Write it on a sticky note. Put it where you will see it throughout the week as a reminder that a life lived prudently puts us on the better path.

† Take time this week to compose a vision statement for your life. Who are you? Where are you going? How will you get there? Let the dreams of your heart take shape in expressing your true identity and your most noble desires. Then commit yourself to reading that statement every week, maybe even sharing it with someone you trust so you can have an accountability partner on your journey.

† Take time this week to read Jesus' Sermon on the Mount in chapters five through seven of St. Matthew's Gospel. These chapters contain a summary of our Lord's teaching about how to live a meaningful life. As you read, highlight the verses that strike you most and reflect prayerfully about why they resonate with you and how you could live better the lessons they teach.

† Write down your typical weekly schedule. Then imagine if you were less prudent than you already are—how would that schedule look? Then imagine that you were more prudent than you are right now—what difference would that make in your typical weekly schedule?

† As the ancient proverb goes: "The way of fools is right in their own eyes, but those who listen to advice are the wise" (Proverbs 12:15). This week, take an older friend or relative out for lunch or a cup of coffee and talk about something meaningful. Give the person a chance to share his or her wisdom and allow yourself a chance to benefit from it.

Chapter 5: *Waiting*

Winter is a season full of waiting. The cold and the dark force us into a certain inaction. We have to wait for the spring thaw before we can return to the baseball diamond and the vegetable garden. Even our impressive technological achievements are often stalled by the implacable powers of winter weather. A mighty snowstorm suavely shuts down even the swankiest schools, effortlessly grounds the largest airplanes, and grinds the busiest cities to a screeching halt. For a time, everyone has to wait it out. We are faced with our smallness, our limits, our vulnerability. "You're not God," the blizzard says. "You must wait."

Winter landscapes are icons of waiting and limitation. Fertile fields reduced to barren plains of white. A stalk of grass peeking through the snowy cloak here and there, powerless against the cold. Majestic trees starkly silhouetted against the slate-gray winter sky, naked and leafless, skeletal and weird. A frozen river exposed and hushed, stilled and silenced by the merciless grip of steely ice, a blank ribbon of white and silver eerily unmoving as it wraps around the hills and valleys.

Winter descends and demands patience; a season full of waiting.

Have you ever reflected on how long a typical person spends waiting? We wait in line almost every day. We wait in traffic. We wait for a response to our college application or our job interview. We wait for the next holiday and the next football game. We wait for our paycheck and our promotion. We wait nine months for the birth of a child and then another two years or so for her to start speaking sentences. We wait for an answer to our prayer for guidance and light. We wait for Christmas to come, for Lent to be over, for vacation to arrive. In a very real sense, we are always waiting for something.

In a culture that idolizes immediate gratification, it's hard for us to wait well. We have to learn the art of waiting—the virtue of patience—intentionally. If we don't, we will always be anxious.

During the last years of my dad's life we spent a lot of time together. Those extended visits were a blessing for our relationship, as I have written about elsewhere in this meditation series. Our love deepened and our companionship became a fount of joy for both of us. But it came at a price.

My dad felt painfully frustrated by his limited activity. He felt useless. He complained sometimes with a tangible, anguished tension. He would say, "I used to be useful. Now I can't do anything. I am useless." It was a heavy burden for him. He had always been a doer to the extreme. A year or two before he retired he took up taekwondo. There he was, a sixty-five-year-old trial attorney, working out with teenagers and learning a whole new world of athleticism.

The winter of his final years was painful, in that sense, but also fruitful. His forced inaction created the space for us to get to know each other and grow closer. Without it, he never would have had an extended season of self-reflection. His penchant for activity would have kept him focused on exterior things. The providential circumstances of his final season forced him to reflect on his past, himself, his life, and the world with a fullness that went beyond his comfort zone. He shifted into a more contemplative mode, to his everlasting benefit. Those wintry last few years allowed his soul to unwind, to relax, in a sense, and to become more open to God—a blessed preparation for the final journey from this life into the next. That period of waiting worked on his heart in such a way that he died under God's mercy.

The key to the art of waiting is faith. Faith is the supernatural certainty that God knows what he is doing, that the seasons he sends us have their purpose, and that each one can contribute to forming us for heaven. Faith enables us to accept the limitations imposed by winter, trusting that in some mysterious way a new springtime is being prepared. Faith even opens our eyes to the beauty of winter, its purity and its power, its noble message that "you are not God," which can bring us much peace if we let it. God is God, and he is on our side, gazing at us with love and showering us with blessings in accordance with his wisdom.

The psalmist has learned the art of waiting; he sees the hand of God at work in our winters and in all the rhythms of the seasons:

> He sends his command to earth;
>> his word runs swiftly!
> Thus he makes the snow like wool,
>> and spreads the frost like ash;
> He disperses hail like crumbs.
> Who can withstand his cold?
> Yet when again he issues his command,
>> it melts them;
>> he raises his winds and the waters flow.
> *Psalm 147:15–18*

The lessons learned from the seasons teach us to wait joyfully, to fill our waiting with trust and love, to do what we can do and to accept what we cannot. And so the stillness of winter can also be filled with the energy of life, through faith:

> Be still before the LORD;
>   wait for him....
> Wait eagerly for the LORD,
>   and keep his way;
> He will raise you up to inherit the earth.
> *Psalm 37:7, 34*

We have to ask ourselves, why is life so full of waiting? Why doesn't everything just happen all at once, in its fullness? Is there a purpose behind these rhythms, these ebbs and flows, these winters strewn throughout every season of our lives? Yes, the rhythms of life have a purpose and a meaning. So does waiting.

Heaven is the fullness of life completely present in an everlasting now, a moment of infinite encounter outside of time and space as we understand it. We are made for heaven. This is why waiting is hard for us. Yet we are also made to make our way toward heaven by traveling responsibly through time. Our lives here on earth unfold gradually, like the seasons, and this is how God wishes to prepare us for the gift of blessedness that comes with heaven. Just as a baby in the womb gradually develops all the organs and structures and abilities that will be needed for life outside the womb, so we develop—if we make responsible use of our freedom—all the spiritual organs and capacities that we will need to enjoy the bliss of everlasting life. God didn't have to make us this way, but he did. We are, as the ancients used to say, *in statu viae:* in a state of journeying, of being "on the way."

All the waiting is meant not to torture us but to teach us, to give us time and space to grow in wisdom, courage, temperance, and love—all the virtues that fit us to receive heavenly joy.

Making It Your Own

† Choose one sentence from this chapter that really resonated in your heart or compose a one-sentence summary. Write it on a sticky note. Put it where you will see it throughout the week as a reminder of how important it is to learn the art of waiting.

† List all the things you are waiting for right now. Also list how waiting for each makes you feel. Then speak to God in prayer about those feelings. Ask God to strengthen your faith and hope so your waiting is fruitful.

† Think of someone you know who is going through a painful period of waiting. Reach out to that person this week, offering encouragement and accompaniment.

† This week, prayerfully reflect on what it must have been like for Jesus, Mary, and Joseph to live a quiet life in Nazareth for thirty years. What did Jesus think about during those years? What was he waiting for? What did Mary think of so many years spent in a normal life when she knew about her Son's higher calling? Write down the thoughts that come to you and try to discover the lessons God wants to teach you through those insights.

† Try to think of someone you know who is an artist of some kind. Reach out to that person this week. Ask the artist about his or her creative process. Try to discover the role that waiting plays in that process. Then write down the thoughts that come to you as a result of that conversation as a way of intentionally learning the art of waiting.

Chapter 6: *Perseverance*

I have never been ice fishing, but this curious winter pastime has long fascinated me. If you are not from the northern climes, you may not be familiar with how it works. The idea is simple. The cold winter temperatures freeze the top of good fishing lakes. Four, six, even eight inches of ice can form as frigid weather settles in. Underneath that slick, solid veneer, the rest of the lake is liquid. Although the metabolism of the fish slows, they don't actually hibernate. They eat less and swim sluggishly, but they are still ready for the catch.

The ice fisherman fills a sled with his equipment. Finding the right spot, he pulls out an ice auger to drill a hole through the ice to the still waters beneath. An ice chisel is then employed to widen the hole to about a foot in diameter. He has to keep his skimmer handy to periodically clear away the slush that forms on the edges of the hole.

The image of the ice fisher says a lot to me. Underneath the frozen and inert surface, the lake still has a living pulse. With a little work, a little determination and perseverance, we can reach down and find it. As a priest, I often run across people whose spiritual lives seem frozen. Nothing transcendent or religious resonates with them. I don't know why, at first. Sometimes their hearts seem to be frozen over by wounds and injustices. Other times their own decisions and sins may have dulled their spiritual sensitivity. In all cases, however, I know that beneath the spiritually frozen surface beats a heart created by God and for God, made by love and for love—eternal, everlasting love.

I didn't grow up Christian. I don't remember going to church or receiving any religious formation until I was thirteen. At that point, my older sister had a conversion. She was born again, became a believer in Jesus, and started going to a nondenominational Christian church. My little sister and I had no interest in what was happening to her. I had no spiritual sensitivity, no faith, and no desire for faith. I didn't even feel a need to explore those things. I loved my school, my sports, my activities—my life was full and promising, and it was enough.

But my older sister wanted to share her new discovery. Around Christmas she talked to us about eternal life and faith in Jesus and whether we even cared if Mom, who had passed away a few years earlier, was in heaven or not. I don't remember the specific words or arguments she used. But I do remember her sincerity. She spoke to us from her heart. Although her arguments didn't convince me to believe, her conviction elicited my respect. I agreed to start going to church with her. She later told me that was the first answer to her constant prayers on my behalf.

I enjoyed my first Sunday service. The congregation was young and energetic. The preaching was stimulating. The youth group, welcoming. I started going regularly. I even joined the youth choir and made new friends. It was fun. It was exciting. But I didn't actually believe.

The choir director asked us to us bow our heads in prayer at the beginning and end of every rehearsal. I never did. I sat in the back and looked around at all those poor people with their heads lowered. If they needed that, OK. But I didn't.

I wasn't a conscious and convinced atheist. Spiritual things just had no resonance with me. My spiritual life was slumbering under a thick layer of ice. I wasn't a believer. I didn't know God. It just didn't matter to me.

My social participation in church continued for six months or so. All the while, my older sister was praying passionately and daily for my spiritual awakening. During one of our choir concerts, her prayers were answered dramatically.

We were singing our final song, "Let There Be Light." The choir platform was in the front of the church. The back wall of the church was decorated with an enormous stained-glass window. It was late afternoon, and the sun was setting. Its spreading rays pierced that window and made the colors come alive. I gazed at them as we sang. In that moment, God touched my heart. His grace drilled a hole through my unconscious indifference and I became a believer. I knew God existed and that he was offering me his friendship through Jesus Christ. Everything I had heard in the past months' sermons clicked. God communicated to me, in some mysterious way, that *I mattered to him* and that there was more to life than I knew. He invited me to follow him on a great adventure. His invitation was good and strong, respectful and true. I couldn't doubt. I said "yes." My faith was stirred to life. I became a Christian.

The next time the communion plate came around, I picked up one of the crackers and participated. And my sister, sitting at my side, saw me do it. She put her arm around me, hugged me close, and started to cry. Her prayers had been answered. She had persevered in faith and hope, doing her best to drop a line through the ice into the cold and sluggish waters beneath. And God had been faithful.

When we look at the evil in the world, the immeasurable suffering and injustice, the endless trail of war and violence, the ever-morphing forms of human trafficking and slavery, the misery of entire populations shackled by the corruption and egoism of power-hungry leaders, the exploitation of the weak by the strong, it is easy to lose hope. It is easy to become discouraged. Tales of hardship and sorrow reach back as far as humanity does. What right do we have to enjoy the good things of life when so many of our brothers and sisters are in dire straits? What possibility do we have of making a real difference in the face of gargantuan and globalized social problems? The fallen world is like spiritually frozen tundra, where love and joy are just brief glints of cold sunlight on a vast lake of deadening, egotistical ice.

Yet God has assured us that even though evil is real, it is only part of the story. Underneath the frozen surface, all that makes life worth living still stirs and breathes. He has promised us that if we drill through the ice and reach into the depths of his love and his wisdom, we will have "life, and have it more abundantly" (John 10:10). He has redeemed this world with his grace, and the messiness of the here and now will eventually transfigure into a new heaven and a new earth, a new order purified of every evil and injustice:

> He will wipe every tear from their eyes, and there shall be no more death or mourning, wailing or pain, [for] the old order has passed away.
>
> *Revelation 21:4*

Perseverance in faith, hope, and love will prove to be the deeper truth, truer than the often-discouraging surface of things in this fallen world. This is the ice fisher's wisdom, a winter jewel free for the taking.

I don't always know what to say to pierce through the apathy or antagonism that keeps a person distant from God. I don't always know how to drill through the ice that surrounds a human heart. But I do know that God is faithful. Because he has made us for himself, every heart is in some way restless and searching until it finds and rests in him. The cold surface of indifference or even of evil may slow the metabolism of our search for spiritual meaning, but it can't stop it completely, not as long as this earthly sojourn lasts.

If we are willing to brave the cold and venture out onto the ice, we are assured, eventually, of making a catch. If we continue to persevere in believing, in hoping, in loving, in praying, somehow we will help break through the ice. Whether it's our own heart that needs to be renewed or someone else's, faith-filled perseverance will always prevail, as our Lord himself promised:

> But the one who perseveres to the end will be saved.
>
> *Matthew 24:13*

Making It Your Own

† Choose one sentence from this chapter that really resonated in your heart or compose a one-sentence summary. Write it on a sticky note. Put it where you will see it throughout the week as a reminder that perseverance points to deeper truth.

† Reflect prayerfully on the people who have believed in you through the years. Savor the strength and goodness that came to you through them. Thank God for them.

† List things that discourage you. Reflect prayerfully on why they are discouraging. Try to see them from God's perspective, in light of the ice fisher's wisdom. Decide how you will deal with those things from now on.

† Is there someone in your life you have given up on? How can you continue to love the individual without being adversely affected by his or her flaws or enabling his or her dysfunctions? Say a prayer entrusting this person to the transforming power of God's grace and give yourself permission to believe that God has heard your prayer.

† Think about the people in your life who are struggling with discouragement right now. Think about how you could reach out to one of them this week with a gesture of encouragement. Write your commitment in your calendar so you remember it.

Chapter 7: *Hope*

Winter teaches us there is a limit to the darkness. The earth rotates on its axis while it orbits the sun, but that axis is tilted. If it were at a perfect right angle with the plane of its orbit, the sun's rays would hit the earth's surface with full force. Some theorists surmise that this would make life on earth impossible. The days would be too hot and the nights would be too cold. As it is, the earth's tilt allows the sun's rays to reach the earth at different angles, depending on the season. The gyroscopic properties of the axial rotation create slight variations within those general angles, allowing for gradual transitions between seasons. When the Northern Hemisphere is leaning away from the sun, because of the earth's tilt, it experiences the season of winter, while the Southern Hemisphere experiences summer, and vice versa.

Scientists can only hypothesize about why the earth rotates on a tilted axis. One theory posits that proto-planets began to form from the solid matter of the solar system under the influence of the sun's gravitational force. These miniplanets then collided, and since the nebulous matter wasn't fully solidified, some of the collisions led to combinations, like two lumps of soft clay being mashed together into one larger lump. Possibly, a late collision of this type tilted the planet's rotational axis.

Whatever the original material cause for this rotation, one spiritual meaning is that there is a limit to the darkness. As autumn advances toward winter, the days get shorter. Fewer and fewer hours of daylight cede to more and more hours of darkness. Around December 22 (for the Northern Hemisphere) the winter solstice claims the longest night of the year, the darkest twenty-four hours of the entire calendar. But after the solstice, instead of a descent into permanent and total darkness, the days begin, little by little, to brighten. Just when our hope was waning, it receives a cosmic boon.

I met a beggar once who had every reason to despair. She was middle-aged and had a horrendous and severely disabling type of palsy. She had only a general command of her limbs. She was standing on the side of the road with a sign asking for donations. We were a few cars behind where she was standing, and the light was red. I rolled down the window and waved her over. We offered her alms, and as she took them from my hand, I noticed a rosary bracelet around her wrist. I told her I liked it, and her eyes lit up. She told me she loved Jesus. I answered I did, too, and I explained that both of us in the car were Catholic priests. At that, she moved a bit closer to the car and asked if she could tell us something—something she had never told anyone. I said she certainly could. She prefaced her story with a coherent disclaimer—although she was extremely disabled, physically speaking, she was not mentally disabled at all. Then she proceeded to describe the one tangible, palpable religious experience she had had in her life.

It occurred when she was much younger. She was attending the dedication of a new church. The ceremony was beautiful and memorable in itself, but something personally extraordinary occurred to her. From the beginning of the Mass she had been graced with a spiritual vision of the Blessed Virgin Mary, who was watching over the celebration and praying for the congregation. At one point, Mary looked at her and smiled.

When she finished her story, she said nothing like that had ever happened again, but the experience stayed fresh in her mind through the years. She explained that she thought about it a lot, that it made everything else OK. Then she looked at me with a somewhat anxious expression and asked me what it meant. Why had that happened to her?

I looked at her and said, "It is very clear why you were granted that amazing grace. God wants you to know that you are loved, that he knows and loves you through and through with the unique tenderness of a mother's heart, and that there is a place in his family in heaven being prepared for you. He wants you to remember all of that, no matter what. That's why he sent the Blessed Virgin Mary to smile at you that day, and that's why he allowed you to see her in such a special way."

Her story struck me deeply and it has stayed with me ever since. She was wiser than me. She knew how to keep the eyes of her heart focused on the light, even in the midst of so much darkness that had come her way. She had learned to obey the advice St. Peter gives in his second New Testament letter, speaking about the message of God's love and plan of salvation in Christ:

> You will do well to be attentive to it, as to a lamp shining in a dark place, until day dawns and the morning star rises in your hearts.
>
> *2 Peter 1:19*

One of the titles given to Jesus in the Bible is "the Light of the World." Saint John describes this at the beginning of his Gospel, drawing out the spiritual significance of the natural phenomena of light and darkness:

> What came to be through [Jesus] was life, and this life was the light of the human race; the light shines in the darkness, and the darkness has not overcome it.
>
> *John 1:3–5*

A passage from the Old Testament offers an even more poetic interpretation of the coming of Jesus into the world, to bring light (truth, mercy goodness, grace, hope) to a world mired in ignorance, lust, injustice, despair, and every form of sin. This prophetic passage is read during the liturgical celebrations at Christmas, the holy day when Christ's birth is celebrated:

> The people who walked in darkness have seen a great light; upon those who dwelt in a land of gloom a light has shone.
>
> *Isaiah 9:1–2*

Historians have no way of knowing with certainty whether December 25, Christmas Day, was the actual birthday of Jesus. Much historical research has gone into understanding the gradual development of that liturgical celebration. But the significance of commemorating the midnight birth of the Savior of the world in the darkest days of Palestine's winter has always been associated with the power of hope. Just as the darkness of winter must gradually recede to allow the brightness of summer to return, so, too, the moral darkness of sin and suffering must recede with the advent of God's saving grace wherever it makes an entrance.

In early Christian art, the symbol for hope was an anchor. The early Christians knew very well that faith in God didn't remove all trouble from life on earth—struggles, persecution, sickness, and death were companions of believers and unbelievers as well. The message of Jesus and his crucifixion and resurrection opened up a wider horizon. It gave knowledge of life beyond this fallen world, a life in which suffering would cease and joy would be unending. God's grace and mercy were available to all to lead every believer through the present darkness into the light of eternal life. This supernatural hope has been a source of heroic courage and hidden strength ever since. As the Book of Hebrews puts it:

Two irrevocable assurances, over which there could be no question of God deceiving us, were to bring firm confidence to us poor wanderers, bidding us cling to the hope we have in view, the anchorage of our souls.

Hebrews 6:18–19,
Knox Translation

An anchor gives stability to a seafaring vessel. It keeps it grounded amid turbulent waters. It's an eloquent symbol of the steadfastness, endurance, and dependability that God's love brings to any human heart who accepts it. No matter how dark things may get, no matter how long the darkness lasts, the light will never be vanquished.

What is your anchor in life? What are you hoping for, and how are you hoping to get it? What hopes do you nourish by mulling them over and calling them to mind? These are important questions. The powers of darkness are real, and they never tire of trying to jade us, to lull us into cynicism, useless criticism, and the deadening spiritual anemia of quiet despair. We need to be convinced that the darkness, the failures, the complications, the messes, and all the tangles of life in this fallen world are not the conclusion of the story. There is, and there always will be, an end to the darkness. This, too, is a lesson to be learned from the wisdom of winter.

Making It Your Own

† Choose one sentence from this chapter that really resonated in your heart or compose a one-sentence summary. Write it on a sticky note. Put it where you will see it throughout the week as a reminder that there is always an end to the darkness.

† Take time this week to list your fondest hopes. Then reflect prayerfully on them, one by one. Which ones have been fulfilled? Which ones have you wisely abandoned? Which ones have you unfairly given up on and what will you do about it?

† Hopelessness expresses itself in many different ways: escaping from reality through compulsive behaviors; always being a wet blanket in the face of others' successes; using sarcasm and criticism as habitual modes of communication. Do a quick "X-ray" of your own emotional and spiritual life. Where and why do despair, pessimism, or cynicism appear? Treat those infections to a powerful dose of prayerful hope.

† This week, reach out to someone going through a dark time. Don't feel you need to rescue the person. But maybe your presence and interest can remind her or him of the light that is sure to come when winter recedes.

† The ancient Christian symbol of hope was an anchor. What is your personal symbol of hope? Spend time prayerfully reflecting on it this week. Also this week, consciously adopt your own symbol of hope.

Chapter 7:
Companionship

The limited outdoor activity allowed by winter weather opens up abundant possibilities to enjoy the simple—and necessary—pleasures of companionship. We tend to spend more time with our family members, work colleagues, and friends. As the outward range of activity contracts, we are faced with an opportunity to expand the inward depths of our more central relationships.

Today's culture, with its many tricks for bypassing the rhythms of the season, may attempt to downplay this tendency, but it can't eliminate it. In wintertime we bundle up more and feel a preference for cuddling next to the fire with a warm drink, a good book, and a pleasant companion.

You even see this dynamic emerge in public places amidst strangers. During a snowstorm that grounds planes and delays flights, airports become arenas of encounter. A fundamental truth of human nature—we are social beings who discover and fulfill our true identities in relationships— breaks out and takes over.

Our need for meaningful relationships is the source of our greatest joys as well as our deepest sorrows. Relationships are essential for our fulfillment, but they are also hard. Our fallen human nature fills us with subconscious fears and prejudices that affect our capacity to relate to others authentically and respectfully. Human maturity consists largely in learning to manage those destructive tendencies to build and maintain healthy relationships. Without developing that maturity, loneliness, regret, and frustration can tyrannize us even in the midst of apparent success and happiness. What is the secret to achieving this maturity? What is the path to growing in respectful openness? I think part of the answer to those questions is contained in the very word companionship.

A companion is someone you share meals with on a regular basis. Eating together brings people into a basic common space and activity that serves as a catalyst for mutual knowledge and growth in intimacy. When we share a meal, we share our presence and our vulnerability.

There is no perfect companion, no perfect friend, no perfect family member. We are all incomplete. And that's OK. It's how we are designed.

In the Northern Hemisphere, the holiday

season coincides with the coming of winter. The weeks of this holiday season are filled to overflowing with banquets, parties, feasts, and shared meals. Most especially, there are the family get-togethers where everyone shares in preparing and enjoying the food. This season-within-a-season is characterized in a special way by companionship, literally and figuratively.

We also know that family get-togethers are not always characterized by unadulterated joy. The dysfunctions at work in our relationships can't hide so well during those times of companionship. The wounds and the unresolved misunderstandings, festering quietly during much of the year, are often exposed and aggravated when we come together to share a common table.

The funny thing is, as children we often experience only the good side of those family get-togethers. At least that's how I remember it. My family used to split the "big three" meals— Thanksgiving, Christmas, and New Year's—among my dad, my uncle, and my grandmother. Every year, each would host all the others with their family members and other companions. How I used to look forward to each gathering! Seeing my cousins, playing games, sitting around with all the adults while they talked and laughed, curiously exploring my uncle's house or my grandmother's apartment building together with my sisters. The food itself was a big attraction, too. I was always hungry as a kid, and on those holidays you basically started eating scrumptious things when you arrived and didn't stop until you left.

I vividly remember sitting at the grownups' table and gazing with fond affection at everyone. I really didn't understand everything they were talking about, but there was my grandmother's wise face, my aunt's sparkling eyes, my uncle's mischievous smile, and my dad's tough but somehow comforting solemnity. It didn't occur to me to criticize them. I just accepted them. And I assumed they just accepted me. We were each unique, of course, but we were each sitting at the same table, companions on a special day. We were all in it together, and that was wonderful, marvelous, delightful.

I have often thought about those experiences now that I am a grownup. Companionship is a simple thing when you are a child. A child's instinct is to accept another person as is and go from there. I wonder if that sense of simple companionship is an ingredient that could help heal and improve all of our relationships.

Plenty of sociological and psychological studies have concluded that the single most helpful behavior for marriages, families, and children who are growing up is sharing a family meal every day. By sitting down at the table together, the natural bonds of companionship we all need to live a fulfilling life are nourished, just as our bodies are nourished by the food we eat. If that truly is the case, it is no wonder that families find it harder and harder to do that. The spiritual forces at work in a post-Christian culture would hardly want to encourage healthy companionship, an essential ingredient in the unfolding of our true identity as created in the image and likeness of God. All the more reason to reclaim this as a priority, to let this morsel of winter wisdom move us in the right direction.

One of my favorite Bible passages has to do with this multifaceted meaning of "companionship." It's from Revelation. In this verse, Jesus opens his heart, showing his fundamental desire, and he also makes a promise. Here is what he says:

> Behold, I stand at the door and knock. If anyone hears my voice and opens the door, [then] I will enter his house and dine with him, and he with me.
>
> *Revelation 3:20*

Jesus stands at the door and knocks. He reveals that God wants to enter our lives. He wants to be part of the gentle conversations in the living room, around the fire. He wants to break bread with us, share our table, sit with us and be present to us. But he knocks. He doesn't break down the door.

The Lord is kind and respectful. He waits for our hospitality, for our willingness to open ourselves up and welcome him, to invite him to sit down with us. If we do invite him in, he promises not only to respect us and to accompany us, but to allow us to know him and accompany him: "I will enter his house and dine with him, and he with me." It is no mistake that in the Church's liturgy, the altar—the place of worship and sacrifice—is also a table, the place of holy Communion.

There is something sacred about true companionship. Something mysterious. Something essential for a meaningful life. But true companionship requires accepting others, letting them be themselves, just as we must accept ourselves. It's a worthy theme for reflection and a valuable virtue to cultivate. After all, God has revealed that the closest thing on earth to help us understand what heaven will be like is a banquet:

> I say to you, many will come from the
> east and the west, and will recline with
> Abraham, Isaac, and Jacob at the banquet
> in the kingdom of heaven.
>
> *Matthew 8:11*

Making It Your Own

† Choose one sentence from this chapter that really resonated in your heart or compose a one-sentence summary. Write it on a sticky note. Put it where you will see it throughout the week as a reminder of the importance of authentic companionship.

† Take time this week to reflect on the role of companionship in your life. What role does it play? What role would you like it to play? What steps can you take to move in the right direction?

† In some cultures, meals together still constitute some of the most meaningful times in life. In other cultures, eating has lost this spiritual dimension. Reflect on the role of having meals together in your and your family's life. How often do you have a meal with companions that you are free to simply enjoy? What are your most important meals each week and why? What changes could you make to live this necessity of life—eating— in a more spiritually and companionably enriching way?

† Think prayerfully about the relationships in your life. Consider the ones you are dissatisfied with. What is the cause of that dissatisfaction? How much of the responsibility do you bear? How much of the responsibility is on the other person's shoulders? Would there be a way forward if you were better able to accept yourself and the other person without unspoken or unreasonable expectations? Ask God to help you see and love other people as he does.

† A get-together with a meal is one of the most common and meaningful ways to celebrate important events and achievements. What significant events in the lives of your family and friends could you celebrate better? Think, for example, of baptismal anniversaries, confirmation anniversaries, saints' days.... What can you do to reassert meaningful traditions like these?

Chapter 9: *Benevolence*

A sunny day in winter may be uncomfortably and inconveniently cold. It can also be brilliantly bright. The air in the sky seems thinner and the sunlight cuts through with a dazzling sharpness. When the ground is covered in a fresh blanket of snow, its reflection intensifies dazzlingly. On days like that, the world has two sources of light: the heavens and the earth. It's almost too magnificent to appreciate. The brightness is almost blinding. If you have to drive anywhere on such a day, bring your sunglasses.

These days are stimulating. Less romantic and comforting than a gray day with a gentle snowfall, the bright "double-sun" days stir you into action. They make you want to do something, to make something. They wake you up. They clear the air of the doldrums and slumbers alike.

As a boy, I had mixed feelings about them. The lazy part of me preferred the hazier days because they lulled you into daydreams and naps. Those bright winter days, on the other hand, spurred me forward and reminded me there is more to life than sipping hot chocolate. They were demanding.

It wasn't always easy responding generously to those demands. Yet it was always worth it.

Love has a side to it very much like those double-bright winter days. Love wants what is truly best for the beloved and won't settle for anything less. If my beloved is underachieving—morally, personally, or spiritually—I cannot endure it. I feel a desire and a duty to stimulate change, to wake that person up and help him or her leave mediocrity behind.

This can be unhealthy if my love is tainted by selfishness, as when emotionally needy parents try to relive (and revise) their own regret-filled youth through their children's achievements. But when it stems from a sincere appreciation for the person in question, from self-forgetful love, it is healthy and can be fruitful. This wanting the very best, the truly best, for another person is the core meaning of an old word with beautiful roots: benevolence.

One of my fondest memories from childhood comes from an incident that may sound insignificant, but it made a lasting impression on me. It was an encounter with my dad's benevolence.

It was a difficult season in my family's life. I was eight or nine years old, a couple years after my parents' divorce. My mother was sick but hadn't yet passed away. My dad hoped to give us a stable home by marrying again, but it didn't work out as he planned. We were in transition. He was looking for a new home, and in the meantime we were living in some former servants' quarters above a stable. We called it the coach house. The stable was part of an estate where one of my dad's friends had grown up. He was helping us until my dad could get things back on track.

The coach house didn't have a kitchen. So my dad cooked for us on one of those old electric skillets. The quarters also didn't have a proper bathroom, so we had to take turns sharing a rusty showerhead attached to a wall in the basement. Each morning after breakfast, my older sister and I took a long walk to the nearest bus stop while my dad dropped off my little sister. He'd pick her up on his way home from work and my older sister would stay late for practices after school. So I was often home alone when I got back from school.

I didn't mind very much. Living on the estate was an adventure. There was a farm, a forest, a huge ravine with a little river running through it, a mansion (off-limits to us), and old barns and warehouses filled with broken-down cars and even an old airplane. I had plenty to explore, and I had my trusty G.I. Joe figure to keep me company.

But I did get lonely sometimes. One day I was completely down in the dumps. I was the only one home. I was sitting on the ground outside the coach house with my baseball glove and a baseball, glum and dejected.

As I wallowed, my dad drove down the driveway. This was a rare occurrence, a schedule anomaly. He parked the car, got out, and said hello. I remember he was dressed in his suit. He had forgotten something and had to pick it up and go back out. He said all this with a goodhearted, fatherly smile. It didn't cheer me up. I don't remember if he asked me how I was feeling, but I am sure he noticed what a blue day I was having.

But then he reemerged from the coach house with a camera. He said something about taking pictures of me for the family photo albums. He started snapping and told me to throw the ball as high as high as I could and catch it when it came down. At first I complied reluctantly, but once he got me going, I started to get into it. We ended up having a great time. Then he had to drive off again, but he promised to drop the film off to get developed. As he drove away I went off to do some exploring with plenty of pep back in my step.

I doubt I would have remembered this encounter if it weren't for the photos. He was true to his word. He had the film developed and then together we put the pictures into one of our family photo albums. Whenever I leaf through the albums I see those photos, an image essay telling the story of that day's journey from sadness to gladness under the wise guidance of my dad. Every time I see the pictures, I replay that entire journey. I feel again the inexplicable melancholy. I remember the warmth coming back into my mind and heart as my dad gave me a healthy dose of love, of attention, of affirmation, of benevolence.

Benevolence has a Latin etymology. It combines *bene* ("well") and *velle* ("want"), meaning to want well or to want what is good. Benevolence is the habitual attitude that truly cares about other people, about what is good for them. The Latin word *velle* implies more than a vague wish. It connotes decision and action. It has the same root that gives us our English *volition* and even, through the arcane paths of linguistic metamorphosis, *will*. A benevolent person is someone who has the warmth of heart to want to help whenever and wherever he can plus the strength of character to act on those desires.

We all need benevolent people. We need folks who are willing to go out of their way to help bring out the best in us. We also need to be benevolent, to care enough about others to engage in their lives respectfully and considerately but also courageously. What hinders us most in our journey through life is a lack of caring, a self-absorbed indifference. Indifferent teachers waste the time we spend under their guidance. Indifferent family members impoverish our lives by depriving us of the enrichment they are called by providence to contribute. An indifferent priest not only fails to inspire others with the life-giving grace of the gospel but he repels them with his counterwitness. When we allow indifference to deaden our spiritual sensitivity, we become less than human, and we feel like it, too.

This attitude of benevolence, of wanting what is truly good for others, whoever they may be, is at the very heart of the gospel. In a sense, the Incarnation of the Son of God was an act of benevolence through which God reached into our damaged world to plant the seed of redeeming grace: "For God so loved the world that he gave his only Son, so that everyone who believes in him might not perish but might have eternal life" (John 3:16). I believe benevolence is at the heart of the golden rule: "Do to others as you would have them do to you" (Luke 6:31). I also believe it is the secret to happiness: "It is more blessed to give than to receive" (Acts 20:35).

Living benevolence isn't easy. It requires us to move out of our comfort zone. It's like that double-bright winter day, not exactly comfortable but stimulating and, in the end, doubly life-giving.

Making It Your Own

† Choose one sentence from this chapter that really resonated in your heart or compose a one-sentence summary. Write it on a sticky note. Put it where you will see it throughout the week as a reminder of the beauty of benevolence.

† Think about the different people who have modeled benevolence throughout your life. Recall some of the times when you were the recipient of their love. Savor those privileged moments, thank God for them, and pray for those people.

† Prayerfully reflect on the different spheres of your life—faith, family, friends, work, hobbies. Take a benevolence "X-ray" of yourself in each of those spheres by reflecting on how easy or hard it is for you to actively seek the good of others in each. You will find that some environments and relationships make it easier to live the golden rule than others. Why is that? Try to discover behavior patterns that can increase your self-knowledge and lead you to grow in benevolence. Ask God to give you the light and the strength you need to make the golden rule into a personal treasure.

† Commit yourself to doing a random act of kindness every day this week. Put it on your calendar. Keep aware of opportunities to do so. At the end of each day, reflect prayerfully on what happened as a result of this commitment and how it made you feel.

† Commit yourself to following through on whatever good deed or gesture has been in your mind and heart for a long time. Maybe it's an act of forgiveness or asking for forgiveness. Maybe it's visiting a relative who lives alone. Maybe it's joining a faith-sharing group at the parish. Whatever it is, accomplish it this week, even if it means stepping out of your comfort zone.

Chapter 10: *Truth*

The frosty air of a chill winter's night is refreshing. After a day spent in the cramped quarters of an office, a workshop, or even a home, cabin fever can begin to dull our wits. Donning boots, a coat, a hat, and a scarf to keep the biting breeze at bay, a walk outside rejuvenates us. After a jaunt through a wintry landscape, our cheeks are flushed and our eyes are bright. The cold jolts our body and stimulates a burst of energy that can clear our minds and even cleanse pent-up emotional turbulence like a natural tonic.

This winter boon is never so evident as during a typical winter pastime like skiing. A few runs over some fresh powder on a lovely winter day revitalize body, mind, and soul. Simpler sports produce the same effect. After a romp in the snowy yard or a session of sledding on the neighborhood hill, kids come back inside fresh-faced and overflowing with chatter, energized by their encounter with winter.

This tonic effect of the cold can even be quantified and measured. Brain performance peaks, some studies say, at the rather unlikely temperature of about forty degrees Fahrenheit. Though such precise measurements can never be flawless, the trend of research clearly indicates that colder temperatures make for hotter thinking.

This has a spiritual parallel. The brisk and sometimes chilling—if not shocking—wind of simple truth—whether moral, existential, or ontological—invigorates us. Truth sets us free—as the Lord explains in John 8:32—from the dull and deadening haze of ambiguity and confusion. It sometimes makes us shiver, but shivering casts off the shackles and tangled knots of sophisms, excuses, evasions, and prevarications we often use to justify our self-inhibiting decisions and self-defeating attitudes. Truth, like the frosty air of a chill winter's night, can be refreshing.

I saw this at work one time, firsthand, in a parking lot. I was coming out of a pharmacy in a mall, winding my way through the many vehicles to my car. I was lost in thought and looked up to see a thirty-something man in a suit and tie running through the lot in my direction. He was running toward me. The look on his face was serious, if not anguished, and a bit alarming. For a moment, I panicked, calculating how long it would take me to put the key in the car door, start the engine, and pull away. But the panic passed, and as he came within speaking distance I said hello.

A bit breathless, he asked politely if he might speak to me for a few minutes. I said, "Of course" and asked what was on his mind. He explained that his mother had recently passed away. The funeral was held about a month ago. He was a Catholic and was trying to live his faith. But his mother had been sick for a long time before her death. It was a sickness that, as it progressed, required more and more assistance to keep the victim alive. He had done his best to accompany her throughout and had arranged for the best medical care he could. But toward the end he made some decisions that he wasn't at peace with. He wasn't sure he had done the right thing. Could I help him understand if he had?

He was almost paralyzed by moral uncertainty. He told me he had been sitting in his car in the parking lot praying for God to help him. When he looked up and saw a priest walking through the lot, he got out of his car and sprinted.

His eyes, his face, his posture, all his nonverbal communicators echoed what he was telling me. I began to ask questions, inviting him to tell me all the details about his mother's sickness, its progress, the steps he had taken—everything.

We stood among the Fords and the Hondas for more than half an hour discussing the case. I was able to identify which decisions were causing him the most distress. As he described the details, it became clear that he had indeed done the right thing, following the Church's teaching about the difference between ordinary and extraordinary means for medical sustenance, which includes the wise distinction between *causing* death and simply *accepting* death. I did my best not to give him false, superficial words of comfort but to help him understand the moral teaching and the wisdom behind it.

As we talked, I could sense—I could almost see—the haze dissipate. As he gradually understood the reasons that made his decisions right and the reasons that would have made other decisions wrong, his anguish visibly diminished. When we were finished, I put out my hand to say goodbye, but instead of shaking hands, he threw his arms around me and gave me a bear hug. He thanked me profusely and then walked calmly and confidently back to his car.

In the Bible, the word *wisdom* often refers to this ability of truth to affect individual lives, even entire societies. Wisdom is where truth and life meet. It is something that all the saints pursued and loved. Even when it stings, like a cold wind

on a frigid winter's day, it revitalizes and refreshes.
That's something all of us can use.

I, Wisdom, dwell with prudence,
 and useful knowledge I have.
Now, children, listen to me;
 happy are they who keep my ways.
Listen to instruction and grow wise,
 do not reject it!
Those who love me I also love,
 and those who seek me find me.
My fruit is better than gold, even
 pure gold
 and my yield than choice silver.
For whoever finds me finds life,
 and wins favor from the LORD;
But those who pass me by do violence
 to themselves;
 all who hate me love death.

Proverbs 8, passim

Making It Your Own

† Choose one sentence from this chapter that really resonated in your heart or compose a one-sentence summary. Write it on a sticky note. Put it where you will see it throughout the week as a reminder that truth refreshes the soul.

† Take time this week to read chapters eight and nine in the Bible's Old Testament Book of Wisdom. Reflect on the message contained in those chapters and turn the prayer for wisdom offered by Solomon in chapter nine into your own prayer.

† List the teachings of the Church that you know about but don't fully understand. Make a commitment to seek a deeper understanding of each of them, even if only by taking little steps each week—asking experts, looking for books and articles, and listening to relevant podcasts.

† This week, reflect prayerfully on where you usually go when you have some doubt or important question that needs to be answered. Are those good places to go? Where else could you look for answers? Where else *should* you go? Commit to open new avenues or to find new resources that can help you in times of need.

† This week, take someone you respect for his or her faith and maturity out to coffee. Talk with that person about how he or she grew in his or her knowledge and wisdom. Try to garner some advice that will be useful in your own ongoing pursuit of growth in this area.

Chapter 11: *Generosity*

As kids, we all learned that every single snowflake is one-of-a-kind. Even recent studies in physics, examining the proto-snow crystals at the nano-level, have confirmed this. Since every snow crystal begins with a cloud droplet, a tiny drop of water, even at that level uniqueness is the norm. This is because when you gather multiple molecules of water together, you inevitably run across some variations on the well-known $H2O$ form. A rogue deuterium atom will masquerade as a hydrogen, for example, or an 18O atom will step in for the usual 16O.

When only a handful of molecules are involved, two proto-snow crystals could in theory be the same, the likelihood, even at that nano-level, is very small. At the microscopic and macroscopic levels, the likelihood approaches zero. Since a macroscopic snow crystal forms as water in a cloud condenses and then freezes on the facets of the original crystal, since the condensation and freezing are affected by the surrounding temperature, and since each individual crystal is bouncing around vigorously throughout the cloud—encountering varying temperatures as it grows—it is virtually impossible for the formation process to be exactly the same in any two cases.

This whole remarkable drama behind the production of a snowflake has led one Caltech physicist to make the following mind-boggling assertion: "It's unlikely that any two complex snow crystals, out of all those made over the entire history of the planet, have ever looked completely alike."

So many trillions of snow crystals forming and falling and melting through the eons of the earth's history, and then forming and falling and melting again, and no two have ever been alike. It defies comprehension. The mind shies away from trying to fathom it. Yet it's true.

When some spiritual experience moves us to begin considering the generous love of God, who creates each individual human soul, who sustains all the forces of the universe that impart and maintain life and beauty and goodness, who never stops thinking about and loving every single one of us, whose mercy is inexhaustible and never-ending— we can find ourselves amazed. We can also balk. *Can God really love me with a personal love? How can that be? Am I not too small and insignificant? Is he not too immeasurable and distant?*

Such questions arise spontaneously in our hearts when we feel an invitation to trust in God's personal love, to believe that we actually matter to him. Knowing ourselves, knowing our limitations and sufferings, our sins and failings, our neediness and woundedness, it seems unlikely the king and Creator of the entire universe would really be interested in our tiny little life.

And yet the fairy tales are, spiritually speaking, true. Cinderella does go to the ball and the prince sees her, notices her, is fascinated and enchanted by her, and sets his whole kingdom in motion to pursue and find her so he can live by her side happily ever after.

The story of Cinderella is the story of the gospel. Jesus is God. He came to earth because he saw us and knew us. He loved us; he was enchanted by each of us and longs to have us at his side now and for all eternity. So full and real is his love for us that he endured poverty and persecution, betrayal and flagellation, injustice and crucifixion and death just to prove that nothing we could ever do will change that passionate, personal, faithful, determined love that he has for you and for me: "I have loved you with an everlasting love....I have engraved you on the palms of my hands" (Jeremiah 31:3; Isaiah 49:16, *English Standard Version*).

It may feel unlikely that God is interested in you and me, just as it would seem unlikely that the earth has never known two snowflakes that are the same. But it is true. God's generosity *is* that big.

I was privileged to get a surprising and uplifting glimpse of generosity at my dad's memorial service. My sisters and I were greeting the guests who had come to the funeral home to pay their respects and offer their condolences. It was a heartwarming affair but also tiring. I was so edified by the people who came: friends and colleagues and past classmates of my dad, old friends, teachers, pastors, and former employers of my sisters and myself. To me, the visitation felt like an array of kindness and a flow of benevolence.

At one point a middle-aged woman whom I had never met introduced herself. She said she had to tell me something, and she was sorry if her presence, as a stranger, was impertinent. I said of course it was not and asked what she wanted to say. She proceeded to tell me a story about something my dad had done, something he had never mentioned.

This woman's sister had lived across the street from my dad for a few years. She and my dad were both divorced, and they became friends over the course of the years when she lived there. My dad would sometimes help with her yard work, and she would bake some scrumptious dessert, or even an entire dinner, when one of us kids would come home for a visit.

She became ill with a strange kind of blood poisoning and died quite suddenly. I remember how surprised I was to hear the news. So was my dad. In fact, everyone was surprised, including her family.

Her sister had to make all the arrangements after her death. She was quite distraught and was juggling a number of difficult situations in her own life. Having to take care of her sister's estate, along with the funeral, was a heavy burden for her.

It turns out that her sister had asked to be buried in the local cemetery but hadn't purchased a plot there. When the sister went to do so, the town declined her. Only town residents were permitted to purchase gravesites in that cemetery. She was distraught—one more complication on top of everything else. She didn't know what to do.

She knew that my dad was an attorney, so she came by to ask for advice. They talked about the situation, and my dad said to her, "Don't worry about it. I'll take care of this." She was relieved and grateful, and she hoped for the best.

My dad did take care of it. He didn't pull any legal strings or barter for an exception. Instead, she found out later, and much to her surprise, he simply purchased the gravesite himself and arranged everything for the burial.

The rush of activity died down and our neighbor's sister finally had a chance to tie up all the loose ends and put things back in order.

Gradually her life went back to normal. Then, later, it dawned on her that she had never received a bill for the gravesite and burial expenses. She followed up and that's when she discovered my dad had done more than simply find a legal solution to her dilemma. She came to the memorial service to tell me that and to express her heartfelt gratitude for his generosity.

It may appear unlikely that history's trillions of snowflakes have each been unique. But it is true. It may appear unlikely that the infinite, all-knowing, all-powerful God is interested—personally and lovingly—in your life and wants you to spend eternity at his side. But it is true, deeply true. And whenever we witness, receive, or perform a genuine act of generosity, we feel the undeniable and unconquerable force and vitality of that truth.

Making It Your Own

† Choose one sentence from this chapter that resonated in your heart or compose a one-sentence summary. Write it on a sticky note. Put it where you will see it throughout the week as a reminder that God's generosity is real.

† Think about people you have known who are particularly generous. Not in the forced, vain way, but in the quiet, wise way. Thank God for them and admire the beauty of that virtue. Imagine how your life would be different if you were to grow in generosity. Write down in a journal the insights that come to you in this exercise.

† Many times we may feel as if we have nothing left to give. That can't be true. At the very least, we can give a prayer, a smile, a word of encouragement, a gesture of affection. Take time this week to read the Gospel story of the Widow's Mite, which you can find in Mark 12:41–44. If you like the story, you may also find it fruitful to spend time reflecting on it by using the *Retreat Guide* at RCSpirituality. org called "The Widow's 'Might.'" Write down the inspirations that come to you as a result of meditating on that passage.

† Think about your commitments and activities scheduled for the coming week. Where is there room or special opportunity for an act of generosity? Make a commitment to perform it and put it in your calendar.

† This week, spend extra time alone with the Lord to give your soul space to experience his love for you in a fresh way. Go to a place where you can usually feel his presence. Bring something along to remind you of his goodness and his goodness to you—your journal, some favorite music, your Bible, a book that has spoken to your heart. When you are there, turn off your phone and rest in the truth that God really is interested in your life, your happiness, and your eternity: "I have loved you with an everlasting love....I have engraved you on the palms of my hands" (Jeremiah 31:3; Isaiah 49:16, *ESV*).

Chapter 12: *Grace*

Throughout these books of meditations I have neglected at least one important aspect of the seasons: their aromas. Each season has its smells. Spring's fresh soil and budding flowers leap with bright and jubilant fragrances. Summer smells are richer and deeper: the dense forest, the freshly cut grass, the growing crops, each wafting its subtle scent into air that can be heavy and humid. Autumn offers its delicious crispness, its nostalgic earthiness as the ground reclaims the empty stalks and fallen leaves. And winter's aromas tend to be more indoor affairs.

The cold air outside is reluctant to communicate a whiff of anything. But those long winter days spent inside, with the crackle of a fire and its mesmerizing woody perfume, with the cooking and the baking having nowhere else to send their tantalizing odors except to the other rooms of the house—yes, winter has its telltale tangs as well.

I shied away from describing these essential characteristics of the seasons precisely because of their poignancy. Describing smells is hard. Describing the effect they have on us is even harder. Some experts say that olfactory memories carry the greatest weight. The smell of a place where something momentous occurred, even if not repeated for a half-century or more, will trigger an emotional replay of the entire experience when encountered again. Such is the power of aroma.

A few years ago, I was praying my rosary on a plane (not my favorite place to be) as we cruised at 30,000 feet. I was in an aisle seat, and in the window seat on my left was an elderly woman. In the middle of my rosary she leaned over and commented, "That's a nice-looking rosary you have there, Father." I don't know what came over me, but without even thinking I responded, "Yes, a priest friend of mine from Jerusalem gave it to me, and it was blessed by the pope. I think you are meant to have it." With that, I took her hand and placed the rosary inside of it. We looked at each other, she a bit shocked and me smiling. She said, "Father, can I ask you a question?" How could I refuse?

She began to tell me about herself and where she was going. Her name was Lois, and she was a practicing and believing Catholic. She was on her way to visit one of her daughters living out west who was having trouble. Back east, where Lois lived, another daughter had recently been divorced, had nowhere to go, and had moved in, bringing her two children with her. That daughter also had some personal issues, and Lois was busy raising her grandkids as well as helping her daughters get their lives in order. It was hard. She was carrying a heavy burden. And it *felt* heavy. She was eighty-something years old and wasn't sure how long she could keep it up.

But that's not what she wanted to talk about. She had something else on her mind. She had been widowed six or seven years earlier after a half-century of a very fulfilling marriage. She missed her husband terribly. She often felt it would be better if she passed away so she could be with him again.

Soon after her daughter and grandchildren moved in with her, a strange thing began to happen. Occasionally, especially when she was taking care of the grandchildren and feeling the burden of life, she would catch the aroma of her favorite flowers, the blooms that had adorned the sanctuary when she had been married, the flowers her husband used to give her every year on their anniversary. Flowers that she never kept around the house anymore.

The first time it happened, she thought it was

just her imagination playing tricks on her. But then it happened again and again. She knew herself to be a practical woman, not a dreamy romantic. And the aroma was so poignant, so real, so unmistakable she simply knew she wasn't imagining it. Besides, if it was just imagination she would turn it on all the time. But she couldn't. When and where it happened was completely out of her control, always a surprise, and always welcome.

"So," she concluded, looking me directly in the eyes, "I am wondering what it means. Can you tell me what it means, Father?"

As I listened to her describing this experience, it was clear she was utterly sincere. In fact, her simple narration of these events moved me deeply. When she asked me to explain what it meant, an answer popped into my mind immediately, as tears formed. "I think," I explained through watery eyes, "I think it's pretty clear what it means. God is giving you a special grace through letting you smell those flowers even when no flowers are around. He wants you to know that even though you feel alone, you aren't alone. He wants you to know that you are still loved and that if he hasn't taken you home to heaven yet, it's for a reason. But the love that sustained you for all these years, the love of your husband and for your husband, a love especially graced by Jesus through the sacrament of marriage, that love is still real and eternal, and you can keep counting on it."

She listened quietly to my answer. When I was finished, while I was wiping my eyes, she patted my arm and smiled at me. Then she looked out the window of the plane and said, "Yep, that's the same thing my parish priest said. So if two priests say the same thing, I guess it must be OK." Then she looked back at me and thanked me for the rosary.

The funny thing about smells is that they don't last very long. If you take a full breath of a rose, the aroma fills your senses dramatically and delightfully, but saturation occurs quickly and the experience seems to fade, though the rose remains.

Something similar occurs in the spiritual life. God sends us significant experiences, encounters, and insights. We feel the significance intensely, but then the feeling subsides and we are left only with the memory. The value of that experience can have a lasting and growing impact on us if we know how to assimilate it, but the sweetness of the moment can be as fleeting as the whiff of orange blossoms carried on a passing breeze.

Spiritual growth involves, among other things, learning to recognize those whiffs of heaven when they come and learning to find the meaning in them. One of the words often used to describe these gifts of God's providence is grace. Its etymological roots are related to a Greek word, *charis*, which is one of St. Paul's favorites. He begins all his New Testament letters by invoking God's grace on his readers.

The word has connotations of loveliness, goodness, winsomeness, and, above all, gratuitousness. A grace is a gift that God gives just because he loves us. There is no hidden agenda. Theologians even use this word to describe the central gift that comes to us in Christ, the gift of sharing the divine life itself, of becoming not just symbolically but truly and mysteriously children of God. Grace is the touch of God that imparts new life and hope to our needy souls. It is the pearl of great price and the treasure buried in the field. It is what makes life worth living.

The beauties and wonders of the seasons are all gifts from God to us. They are all whiffs of divine goodness, living graces that God sends to convince us of his love, his interest in us, his wise plans for the world and for our lives. When we give ourselves the time, the space, and the permission to welcome and savor them, to let them penetrate and inspire us, then we, too, can become living graces for those around us. We also can spread faith, hope, courage, and every good thing, fulfilling our highest calling—that of imaging God here on earth, of becoming, as St. Paul put it, "the pleasing aroma of Christ among those who are being saved" (2 Corinthians 2:15, *NIV*).

Making It Your Own

†   Choose one sentence from this chapter that really resonated in your heart or compose a one-sentence summary. Write it on a sticky note. Put it where you will see it throughout the week as a reminder that God's grace abounds and gives our lives the meaning we crave.

†   Throughout the week, when you find yourself in different places, close your eyes for a few seconds and pay attention to the other sensory stimuli that come to you. Exercise the senses you tend to use less often, becoming more aware of the rich fabric of reality God has given to us. Do this exercise at least once every day for a week and thank God for the experience it grants you.

†   Take time this week to prayerfully reflect on the graces you are most grateful for. List them, describe them in your journal, savor them, and thank God for them.

† Take time this week to prayerfully reflect on the moments in which God has sent graces to others through you. List the most notable of them, describe them in your journal, savor them, and thank God for them.

† Take time this week to prayerfully reflect on the following question: If I could change one thing in my life to make it more grace-filled, what would it be? Ask God to enlighten you, and then pray and think about it. Don't rush to an answer. Let the thoughts that come linger and see which ones settle. By the end of the week, make a decision about what you will do as a result of this interior self-reflection. Speak with a trusted friend or mentor about the decision before you make it final.

About the Author

Fr. John Bartunek, LC, SThD, splits his time between Michigan, where he continues his writing apostolate and assists at Our Lady Queen of the Family Retreat Center in Oxford, and Rome, where he teaches theology at the Pontifical Athenaeum Regina Apostolorum. He is the author of several books, including *The Better Part* and *Inside the Passion: An Insider's Look at the Passion of the Christ.* Fr. Bartunek became a member of the Catholic Church in 1991, was ordained a Catholic priest in 2003, and earned his doctorate in moral theology in 2010. His online retreats are available at **RCSpirituality.org**, and he answers questions about the spiritual life at **SpiritualDirection.com**.